IF FOUND, THIS JOURNAL BELONGS TO:

_____

INSERT NAME

Greetings,

Thank you for taking that big step to purchase this gratitude and self-reflection journal. I realize you had many options to choose from and you chose this one.

This guided journal aims to help you decide what to write while reflecting upon your day. It's okay to take a few minutes to think about the thoughts and emotions that guided your actions. Taking time to acknowledge this leads to self-awareness and gives insight into what you are doing well and where adjustments can be made in your daily life.

Moreover, this gratitude journal helps you to see the goodness around you and within you.

Being mindful that there is something to always be thankful for will keep you aware of the goodness and kindheartedness that still exists in this world that some people overlook.

Take your time as you reflect upon your days in this 90-day gratitude journal. You'll see just how much of a difference acknowledging your thoughts, feelings, and emotions (and being thankful) will make in your life.

Kinyatta

"ACKNOWLEDGING THE GOOD THAT YOU ALREADY HAVE IN YOU IS THE FOUNDATION FOR ALL ABUNDANCE."

~Eckhart Tolle

GRATITUDE CHECKLIST

- ☐ I am thankful for my mind, body and spirit

- ☐ I am thankful for how I generate income and financial independence

- ☐ I am thankful for the relationships I have with family members and friends

- ☐ I am thankful for a companion, spouse, or significant other to share my life with

- ☐ I am thankful for my creativity and extraordinary talents

- ☐ I am thankful for others who perform services (dry cleaners, Uber drivers, etc.) that add convenience to my life

- ☐ I am thankful for the lessons I learn daily

- ☐ I am thankful for the autonomy to make critical life decisions

- ☐ I am thankful for having a reason to smile every day

- ☐ I am thankful for those who trust and believe in me

7-DAYS OF GRATITUDE

SUNDAY
"Learn to be thankful for what you already have as you pursue all that you want." ~Jim Rohn

MONDAY
"This is a wonderful day. I've never seen this one before."
~ Maya Angelou

TUESDAY
"If a fella isn't thankful for what he's got, he's not going to be thankful for what he's going to get." ~Frank A. Clark

WEDNESDAY
"When you are grateful, fear disappears and abundance appears." ~Tony Robbins

THURSDAY
"Thanks for loving me despite my flaws." ~UNKNOWN

FRIDAY
"When I started counting my blessings, my whole life turned around." ~Willie Nelson

SATURDAY
"A thankful heart is not only the greatest virtue, but the parent of all other virtues." ~Cicero

DESCRIBE YOURSELF IN 30 WORDS.

1. _____
2. _____
3. _____
4. _____
5. _____
6. _____
7. _____
8. _____
9. _____
10. _____
11. _____
12. _____
13. _____
14. _____
15. _____

16. _____
17. _____
18. _____
19. _____
20. _____
21. _____
22. _____
23. _____
24. _____
25. _____
26. _____
27. _____
28. _____
29. _____
30. _____

"EMOTIONS HAVE NO GENDER. DON'T LOCK YOURS IN THE DARK."

~Self Esteem Team

THOUGHTS ABOUT ENTREPRENEURSHIP/ CAREER/EDUCATION...

THOUGHTS ABOUT ENTREPRENEURSHIP/ CAREER/EDUCATION...

_____
_____
_____
_____
_____
_____
_____
_____
_____
_____
_____
_____
_____
_____
_____
_____
_____
_____
_____
_____
_____
_____
_____
_____

THOUGHTS ABOUT ENTREPRENEURSHIP/ CAREER/EDUCATION...

THOUGHTS ABOUT MY FAMILY & CHILDHOOD...

THOUGHTS ABOUT MY FAMILY & CHILDHOOD...

_____

_____

_____

_____

_____

_____

_____

_____

_____

_____

_____

_____

_____

_____

_____

_____

_____

_____

_____

THOUGHTS ABOUT MY FAMILY & CHILDHOOD...

THOUGHTS ABOUT MY COMPANION/ SIGNIFICANT OTHER/LIFE PARTNER AND MARRIAGE...

_____

_____

_____

_____

_____

_____

_____

_____

_____

_____

_____

_____

_____

_____

_____

_____

_____

_____

_____

THOUGHTS ABOUT MY COMPANION/ SIGNIFICANT OTHER/LIFE PARTNER AND MARRIAGE...

_____
_____
_____
_____
_____
_____
_____
_____
_____
_____
_____
_____
_____
_____
_____
_____
_____
_____
_____

THOUGHTS ABOUT MY COMPANION/ SIGNIFICANT OTHER/LIFE PARTNER AND MARRIAGE...

_____

_____

_____

_____

_____

_____

_____

_____

_____

_____

_____

_____

_____

_____

_____

_____

_____

_____

_____

_____

_____

THOUGHTS ABOUT RAISING CHILDREN AND/ OR STARTING A FAMILY...

THOUGHTS ABOUT RAISING CHILDREN AND/ OR STARTING A FAMILY...

_____

_____

_____

_____

_____

_____

_____

_____

_____

_____

_____

_____

_____

_____

_____

_____

_____

_____

_____

_____

THOUGHTS ABOUT RAISING CHILDREN AND/ OR STARTING A FAMILY...

THOUGHTS ABOUT MY HOMIES AND ASSOCIATES...

THOUGHTS ABOUT MY HOMIES AND ASSOCIATES...

_____
_____
_____
_____
_____
_____
_____
_____
_____
_____
_____
_____
_____
_____
_____
_____
_____
_____
_____
_____
_____
_____

THOUGHTS ABOUT MY HOMIES AND ASSOCIATES...

I'M FRUSTRATED BY...

_____

_____

_____

_____

_____

_____

_____

_____

_____

_____

_____

_____

_____

_____

_____

_____

_____

_____

_____

_____

I'M FRUSTRATED BY...

_____

_____

_____

_____

_____

_____

_____

_____

_____

_____

_____

_____

_____

_____

_____

_____

_____

_____

_____

I'M FRUSTRATED BY...

_____

_____

_____

_____

_____

_____

_____

_____

_____

_____

_____

_____

_____

_____

_____

_____

_____

_____

_____

LEAVING A LEGACY

Are you living your life in the way that you want to be remembered?

_____

_____

_____

What would you change?

_____

_____

_____

What will you continue doing?

_____

_____

_____

Who's lives have you touched?

_____

_____

_____

90-DAYS OF SELF-REFLECTIONS

Date: /   /

When I need support, I can count on...	Today I Feel:
	☐ Optimistic
	☐ Happy
I felt inspired when...	☐ Sad/Tearful
	☐ Uneasy
	☐ Frustrated
I felt happiest when...	☐ Lonely
	☐ Anger
	☐ Tired

I am grateful for...

I felt disrespected/stressed when...

I spoke up when...

I could have done this better...

I know I'm the "man" when...

This was hard but I overcame it by...

The one thing I will do differently tomorrow is...

This is what I will remember most about today:

90-DAYS OF SELF-REFLECTIONS

Date: /   /

When I need support, I can count on...	**Today I Feel:**
	☐ Optimistic
	☐ Happy
I felt inspired when...	☐ Sad/Tearful
	☐ Uneasy
	☐ Frustrated
I felt happiest when...	☐ Lonely
	☐ Anger
	☐ Tired

I am grateful for...

I felt disrespected/stressed when...

I spoke up when...

I could have done this better...

I know I'm the "man" when...

This was hard but I overcame it by...

The one thing I will do differently tomorrow is...

This is what I will remember most about today:

90-DAYS OF SELF-REFLECTIONS

Date: /   /

	Today I Feel:
When I need support, I can count on...	☐ Optimistic
	☐ Happy
I felt inspired when...	☐ Sad/Tearful
	☐ Uneasy
	☐ Frustrated
I felt happiest when...	☐ Lonely
	☐ Anger
	☐ Tired

I am grateful for...

I felt disrespected/stressed when...

I spoke up when...

I could have done this better...

I know I'm the "man" when...

This was hard but I overcame it by...

The one thing I will do differently tomorrow is...

This is what I will remember most about today:

90-DAYS OF SELF-REFLECTIONS

Date: /   /

	Today I Feel:
When I need support, I can count on...	☐ Optimistic
	☐ Happy
I felt inspired when...	☐ Sad/Tearful
	☐ Uneasy
	☐ Frustrated
I felt happiest when...	☐ Lonely
	☐ Anger
	☐ Tired

I am grateful for...

I felt disrespected/stressed when...

I spoke up when...

I could have done this better...

I know I'm the "man" when...

This was hard but I overcame it by...

The one thing I will do differently tomorrow is...

This is what I will remember most about today:

90-DAYS OF SELF-REFLECTIONS

Date: /   /

When I need support, I can count on...	**Today I Feel:**
	☐ Optimistic
	☐ Happy
I felt inspired when...	☐ Sad/Tearful
	☐ Uneasy
	☐ Frustrated
I felt happiest when...	☐ Lonely
	☐ Anger
	☐ Tired

I am grateful for...

I felt disrespected/stressed when...

I spoke up when...

I could have done this better...

I know I'm the "man" when...

This was hard but I overcame it by...

The one thing I will do differently tomorrow is...

This is what I will remember most about today:

90-DAYS OF SELF-REFLECTIONS

Date: / /

	Today I Feel:
When I need support, I can count on...	☐ Optimistic ☐ Happy
I felt inspired when...	☐ Sad/Tearful ☐ Uneasy ☐ Frustrated
I felt happiest when...	☐ Lonely ☐ Anger ☐ Tired

I am grateful for...

I felt disrespected/stressed when...

I spoke up when...

I could have done this better...

I know I'm the "man" when...

This was hard but I overcame it by...

The one thing I will do differently tomorrow is...

This is what I will remember most about today:

90-DAYS OF SELF-REFLECTIONS

Date: /   /

	Today I Feel:
When I need support, I can count on...	☐ Optimistic
	☐ Happy
I felt inspired when...	☐ Sad/Tearful
	☐ Uneasy
	☐ Frustrated
I felt happiest when...	☐ Lonely
	☐ Anger
	☐ Tired

I am grateful for...

I felt disrespected/stressed when...

I spoke up when...

I could have done this better...

I know I'm the "man" when...

This was hard but I overcame it by...

The one thing I will do differently tomorrow is...

This is what I will remember most about today:

90-DAYS OF SELF-REFLECTIONS

Date: /   /

When I need support, I can count on...	**Today I Feel:**
	☐ Optimistic
	☐ Happy
I felt inspired when...	☐ Sad/Tearful
	☐ Uneasy
	☐ Frustrated
I felt happiest when...	☐ Lonely
	☐ Anger
	☐ Tired

I am grateful for...

I felt disrespected/stressed when...

I spoke up when...

I could have done this better...

I know I'm the "man" when...

This was hard but I overcame it by...

The one thing I will do differently tomorrow is...

This is what I will remember most about today:

90-DAYS OF SELF-REFLECTIONS

Date: /   /

	Today I Feel:
When I need support, I can count on...	☐ Optimistic
	☐ Happy
I felt inspired when...	☐ Sad/Tearful
	☐ Uneasy
	☐ Frustrated
I felt happiest when...	☐ Lonely
	☐ Anger
	☐ Tired

I am grateful for...

I felt disrespected/stressed when...

I spoke up when...

I could have done this better...

I know I'm the "man" when...

This was hard but I overcame it by...

The one thing I will do differently tomorrow is...

This is what I will remember most about today:

90-DAYS OF SELF-REFLECTIONS

Date: ___ / ___ / ___

	Today I Feel:
When I need support, I can count on...	☐ Optimistic
	☐ Happy
I felt inspired when...	☐ Sad/Tearful
	☐ Uneasy
	☐ Frustrated
I felt happiest when...	☐ Lonely
	☐ Anger
	☐ Tired

I am grateful for...

I felt disrespected/stressed when...

I spoke up when...

I could have done this better...

I know I'm the "man" when...

This was hard but I overcame it by...

The one thing I will do differently tomorrow is...

This is what I will remember most about today:

90-DAYS OF SELF-REFLECTIONS

Date: /   /

When I need support, I can count on...	Today I Feel:
	☐ Optimistic
	☐ Happy
I felt inspired when...	☐ Sad/Tearful
	☐ Uneasy
	☐ Frustrated
I felt happiest when...	☐ Lonely
	☐ Anger
	☐ Tired

I am grateful for...

I felt disrespected/stressed when...

I spoke up when...

I could have done this better...

I know I'm the "man" when...

This was hard but I overcame it by...

The one thing I will do differently tomorrow is...

This is what I will remember most about today:

90-DAYS OF SELF-REFLECTIONS

Date: /   /

	Today I Feel:
When I need support, I can count on...	☐ Optimistic
	☐ Happy
I felt inspired when...	☐ Sad/Tearful
	☐ Uneasy
	☐ Frustrated
I felt happiest when...	☐ Lonely
	☐ Anger
	☐ Tired

I am grateful for...

I felt disrespected/stressed when...

I spoke up when...

I could have done this better...

I know I'm the "man" when...

This was hard but I overcame it by...

The one thing I will do differently tomorrow is...

This is what I will remember most about today:

90-DAYS OF SELF-REFLECTIONS

Date: /   /

When I need support, I can count on...	**Today I Feel:**
	☐ Optimistic
	☐ Happy
I felt inspired when...	☐ Sad/Tearful
	☐ Uneasy
	☐ Frustrated
I felt happiest when...	☐ Lonely
	☐ Anger
	☐ Tired

I am grateful for...

I felt disrespected/stressed when...

I spoke up when...

I could have done this better...

I know I'm the "man" when...

This was hard but I overcame it by...

The one thing I will do differently tomorrow is...

This is what I will remember most about today:

90-DAYS OF SELF-REFLECTIONS

Date: /   /

	Today I Feel:
When I need support, I can count on...	☐ Optimistic ☐ Happy
I felt inspired when...	☐ Sad/Tearful ☐ Uneasy ☐ Frustrated
I felt happiest when...	☐ Lonely ☐ Anger ☐ Tired

I am grateful for...

I felt disrespected/stressed when...

I spoke up when...

I could have done this better...

I know I'm the "man" when...

This was hard but I overcame it by...

The one thing I will do differently tomorrow is...

This is what I will remember most about today:

90-DAYS OF SELF-REFLECTIONS

Date: /   /

	Today I Feel:
When I need support, I can count on...	☐ Optimistic
	☐ Happy
I felt inspired when...	☐ Sad/Tearful
	☐ Uneasy
	☐ Frustrated
I felt happiest when...	☐ Lonely
	☐ Anger
	☐ Tired

I am grateful for...

I felt disrespected/stressed when...

I spoke up when...

I could have done this better...

I know I'm the "man" when...

This was hard but I overcame it by...

The one thing I will do differently tomorrow is...

This is what I will remember most about today:

90-DAYS OF SELF-REFLECTIONS

Date: / /

When I need support, I can count on...	**Today I Feel:**
	☐ Optimistic
	☐ Happy
I felt inspired when...	☐ Sad/Tearful
	☐ Uneasy
	☐ Frustrated
I felt happiest when...	☐ Lonely
	☐ Anger
	☐ Tired

I am grateful for...

I felt disrespected/stressed when...

I spoke up when...

I could have done this better...

I know I'm the "man" when...

This was hard but I overcame it by...

The one thing I will do differently tomorrow is...

This is what I will remember most about today:

90-DAYS OF SELF-REFLECTIONS

Date: /   /

When I need support, I can count on...	**Today I Feel:** ☐ Optimistic ☐ Happy
I felt inspired when...	☐ Sad/Tearful ☐ Uneasy ☐ Frustrated
I felt happiest when...	☐ Lonely ☐ Anger ☐ Tired

I am grateful for...

I felt disrespected/stressed when...

I spoke up when...

I could have done this better...

I know I'm the "man" when...

This was hard but I overcame it by...

The one thing I will do differently tomorrow is...

This is what I will remember most about today:

90-DAYS OF SELF-REFLECTIONS

Date: /   /

	Today I Feel:
When I need support, I can count on...	☐ Optimistic ☐ Happy
I felt inspired when...	☐ Sad/Tearful ☐ Uneasy ☐ Frustrated
I felt happiest when...	☐ Lonely ☐ Anger ☐ Tired

I am grateful for...

I felt disrespected/stressed when...

I spoke up when...

I could have done this better...

I know I'm the "man" when...

This was hard but I overcame it by...

The one thing I will do differently tomorrow is...

This is what I will remember most about today:

90-DAYS OF SELF-REFLECTIONS

Date: /   /

	Today I Feel:
When I need support, I can count on...	☐ Optimistic
	☐ Happy
I felt inspired when...	☐ Sad/Tearful
	☐ Uneasy
	☐ Frustrated
I felt happiest when...	☐ Lonely
	☐ Anger
	☐ Tired

I am grateful for...

I felt disrespected/stressed when...

I spoke up when...

I could have done this better...

I know I'm the "man" when...

This was hard but I overcame it by...

The one thing I will do differently tomorrow is...

This is what I will remember most about today:

90-DAYS OF SELF-REFLECTIONS

Date: /   /

When I need support, I can count on...	**Today I Feel:**
	☐ Optimistic
	☐ Happy
I felt inspired when...	☐ Sad/Tearful
	☐ Uneasy
	☐ Frustrated
I felt happiest when...	☐ Lonely
	☐ Anger
	☐ Tired

I am grateful for...

I felt disrespected/stressed when...

I spoke up when...

I could have done this better...

I know I'm the "man" when...

This was hard but I overcame it by...

The one thing I will do differently tomorrow is...

This is what I will remember most about today:

90-DAYS OF SELF-REFLECTIONS

Date: /   /

	Today I Feel:
When I need support, I can count on...	☐ Optimistic ☐ Happy
I felt inspired when...	☐ Sad/Tearful ☐ Uneasy ☐ Frustrated
I felt happiest when...	☐ Lonely ☐ Anger ☐ Tired

I am grateful for...

I felt disrespected/stressed when...

I spoke up when...

I could have done this better...

I know I'm the "man" when...

This was hard but I overcame it by...

The one thing I will do differently tomorrow is...

This is what I will remember most about today:

90-DAYS OF SELF-REFLECTIONS

Date: /   /

When I need support, I can count on...	**Today I Feel:**
	☐ Optimistic
	☐ Happy
I felt inspired when...	☐ Sad/Tearful
	☐ Uneasy
	☐ Frustrated
I felt happiest when...	☐ Lonely
	☐ Anger
	☐ Tired

I am grateful for...

I felt disrespected/stressed when...

I spoke up when...

I could have done this better...

I know I'm the "man" when...

This was hard but I overcame it by...

The one thing I will do differently tomorrow is...

This is what I will remember most about today:

90-DAYS OF SELF-REFLECTIONS

Date: /   /

	Today I Feel:
When I need support, I can count on...	☐ Optimistic
	☐ Happy
I felt inspired when...	☐ Sad/Tearful
	☐ Uneasy
	☐ Frustrated
I felt happiest when...	☐ Lonely
	☐ Anger
	☐ Tired

I am grateful for...

I felt disrespected/stressed when...

I spoke up when...

I could have done this better...

I know I'm the "man" when...

This was hard but I overcame it by...

The one thing I will do differently tomorrow is...

This is what I will remember most about today:

90-DAYS OF SELF-REFLECTIONS

Date: /   /

When I need support, I can count on...	**Today I Feel:**
	☐ Optimistic
	☐ Happy
I felt inspired when...	☐ Sad/Tearful
	☐ Uneasy
	☐ Frustrated
I felt happiest when...	☐ Lonely
	☐ Anger
	☐ Tired

I am grateful for...

I felt disrespected/stressed when...

I spoke up when...

I could have done this better...

I know I'm the "man" when...

This was hard but I overcame it by...

The one thing I will do differently tomorrow is...

This is what I will remember most about today:

90-DAYS OF SELF-REFLECTIONS

Date: / /

	Today I Feel:
When I need support, I can count on...	☐ Optimistic ☐ Happy
I felt inspired when...	☐ Sad/Tearful ☐ Uneasy ☐ Frustrated
I felt happiest when...	☐ Lonely ☐ Anger ☐ Tired

I am grateful for...

I felt disrespected/stressed when...

I spoke up when...

I could have done this better...

I know I'm the "man" when...

This was hard but I overcame it by...

The one thing I will do differently tomorrow is...

This is what I will remember most about today:

90-DAYS OF SELF-REFLECTIONS

Date: ___ / ___ / ___

	Today I Feel:
When I need support, I can count on...	☐ Optimistic ☐ Happy
I felt inspired when...	☐ Sad/Tearful ☐ Uneasy ☐ Frustrated
I felt happiest when...	☐ Lonely ☐ Anger ☐ Tired

I am grateful for...

I felt disrespected/stressed when...

I spoke up when...

I could have done this better...

I know I'm the "man" when...

This was hard but I overcame it by...

The one thing I will do differently tomorrow is...

This is what I will remember most about today:

90-DAYS OF SELF-REFLECTIONS

Date: /   /

When I need support, I can count on...	**Today I Feel:**
	☐ Optimistic
	☐ Happy
I felt inspired when...	☐ Sad/Tearful
	☐ Uneasy
	☐ Frustrated
I felt happiest when...	☐ Lonely
	☐ Anger
	☐ Tired

I am grateful for...

I felt disrespected/stressed when...

I spoke up when...

I could have done this better...

I know I'm the "man" when...

This was hard but I overcame it by...

The one thing I will do differently tomorrow is...

This is what I will remember most about today:

90-DAYS OF SELF-REFLECTIONS

Date: /   /

	Today I Feel:
When I need support, I can count on...	☐ Optimistic
	☐ Happy
I felt inspired when...	☐ Sad/Tearful
	☐ Uneasy
	☐ Frustrated
I felt happiest when...	☐ Lonely
	☐ Anger
	☐ Tired

I am grateful for...

I felt disrespected/stressed when...

I spoke up when...

I could have done this better...

I know I'm the "man" when...

This was hard but I overcame it by...

The one thing I will do differently tomorrow is...

This is what I will remember most about today:

90-DAYS OF SELF-REFLECTIONS

Date: /   /

When I need support, I can count on...	Today I Feel:
	☐ Optimistic
	☐ Happy
I felt inspired when...	☐ Sad/Tearful
	☐ Uneasy
	☐ Frustrated
I felt happiest when...	☐ Lonely
	☐ Anger
	☐ Tired

I am grateful for...

I felt disrespected/stressed when...

I spoke up when...

I could have done this better...

I know I'm the "man" when...

This was hard but I overcame it by...

The one thing I will do differently tomorrow is...

This is what I will remember most about today:

90-DAYS OF SELF-REFLECTIONS

Date: /   /

When I need support, I can count on...	**Today I Feel:**
	☐ Optimistic
	☐ Happy
I felt inspired when...	☐ Sad/Tearful
	☐ Uneasy
	☐ Frustrated
I felt happiest when...	☐ Lonely
	☐ Anger
	☐ Tired

I am grateful for...

I felt disrespected/stressed when...

I spoke up when...

I could have done this better...

I know I'm the "man" when...

This was hard but I overcame it by...

The one thing I will do differently tomorrow is...

This is what I will remember most about today:

90-DAYS OF SELF-REFLECTIONS

Date: /   /

When I need support, I can count on...	Today I Feel:
	☐ Optimistic
	☐ Happy
I felt inspired when...	☐ Sad/Tearful
	☐ Uneasy
	☐ Frustrated
I felt happiest when...	☐ Lonely
	☐ Anger
	☐ Tired

I am grateful for...

I felt disrespected/stressed when...

I spoke up when...

I could have done this better...

I know I'm the "man" when...

This was hard but I overcame it by...

The one thing I will do differently tomorrow is...

This is what I will remember most about today:

90-DAYS OF SELF-REFLECTIONS

Date: /   /

When I need support, I can count on...	**Today I Feel:**
	☐ Optimistic
	☐ Happy
I felt inspired when...	☐ Sad/Tearful
	☐ Uneasy
	☐ Frustrated
I felt happiest when...	☐ Lonely
	☐ Anger
	☐ Tired

I am grateful for...

I felt disrespected/stressed when...

I spoke up when...

I could have done this better...

I know I'm the "man" when...

This was hard but I overcame it by...

The one thing I will do differently tomorrow is...

This is what I will remember most about today:

90-DAYS OF SELF-REFLECTIONS

Date: /   /

	Today I Feel:
When I need support, I can count on...	☐ Optimistic ☐ Happy
I felt inspired when...	☐ Sad/Tearful ☐ Uneasy ☐ Frustrated
I felt happiest when...	☐ Lonely ☐ Anger ☐ Tired

I am grateful for...

I felt disrespected/stressed when...

I spoke up when...

I could have done this better...

I know I'm the "man" when...

This was hard but I overcame it by...

The one thing I will do differently tomorrow is...

This is what I will remember most about today:

90-DAYS OF SELF-REFLECTIONS

Date: /   /

	Today I Feel:
When I need support, I can count on...	☐ Optimistic
	☐ Happy
I felt inspired when...	☐ Sad/Tearful
	☐ Uneasy
	☐ Frustrated
I felt happiest when...	☐ Lonely
	☐ Anger
	☐ Tired

I am grateful for...

I felt disrespected/stressed when...

I spoke up when...

I could have done this better...

I know I'm the "man" when...

This was hard but I overcame it by...

The one thing I will do differently tomorrow is...

This is what I will remember most about today:

90-DAYS OF SELF-REFLECTIONS

Date: /   /

When I need support, I can count on...	**Today I Feel:**
	☐ Optimistic
	☐ Happy
I felt inspired when...	☐ Sad/Tearful
	☐ Uneasy
	☐ Frustrated
I felt happiest when...	☐ Lonely
	☐ Anger
	☐ Tired

I am grateful for...

I felt disrespected/stressed when...

I spoke up when...

I could have done this better...

I know I'm the "man" when...

This was hard but I overcame it by...

The one thing I will do differently tomorrow is...

This is what I will remember most about today:

90-DAYS OF SELF-REFLECTIONS

Date: /   /

	Today I Feel:
When I need support, I can count on...	☐ Optimistic
	☐ Happy
I felt inspired when...	☐ Sad/Tearful
	☐ Uneasy
	☐ Frustrated
I felt happiest when...	☐ Lonely
	☐ Anger
	☐ Tired

I am grateful for...

I felt disrespected/stressed when...

I spoke up when...

I could have done this better...

I know I'm the "man" when...

This was hard but I overcame it by...

The one thing I will do differently tomorrow is...

This is what I will remember most about today:

90-DAYS OF SELF-REFLECTIONS

Date: /   /

	Today I Feel:
When I need support, I can count on...	☐ Optimistic
	☐ Happy
I felt inspired when...	☐ Sad/Tearful
	☐ Uneasy
	☐ Frustrated
I felt happiest when...	☐ Lonely
	☐ Anger
	☐ Tired

I am grateful for...

I felt disrespected/stressed when...

I spoke up when...

I could have done this better...

I know I'm the "man" when...

This was hard but I overcame it by...

The one thing I will do differently tomorrow is...

This is what I will remember most about today:

90-DAYS OF SELF-REFLECTIONS

Date: /   /

	Today I Feel:
When I need support, I can count on...	☐ Optimistic ☐ Happy
I felt inspired when...	☐ Sad/Tearful ☐ Uneasy ☐ Frustrated
I felt happiest when...	☐ Lonely ☐ Anger ☐ Tired

I am grateful for...

I felt disrespected/stressed when...

I spoke up when...

I could have done this better...

I know I'm the "man" when...

This was hard but I overcame it by...

The one thing I will do differently tomorrow is...

This is what I will remember most about today:

90-DAYS OF SELF-REFLECTIONS

Date: /   /

When I need support, I can count on...	Today I Feel:
	☐ Optimistic
	☐ Happy
I felt inspired when...	☐ Sad/Tearful
	☐ Uneasy
	☐ Frustrated
I felt happiest when...	☐ Lonely
	☐ Anger
	☐ Tired

I am grateful for...

I felt disrespected/stressed when...

I spoke up when...

I could have done this better...

I know I'm the "man" when...

This was hard but I overcame it by...

The one thing I will do differently tomorrow is...

This is what I will remember most about today:

90-DAYS OF SELF-REFLECTIONS

Date: /   /

	Today I Feel:
When I need support, I can count on...	☐ Optimistic
	☐ Happy
I felt inspired when...	☐ Sad/Tearful
	☐ Uneasy
	☐ Frustrated
I felt happiest when...	☐ Lonely
	☐ Anger
	☐ Tired

I am grateful for...

I felt disrespected/stressed when...

I spoke up when...

I could have done this better...

I know I'm the "man" when...

This was hard but I overcame it by...

The one thing I will do differently tomorrow is...

This is what I will remember most about today:

90-DAYS OF SELF-REFLECTIONS

Date: /   /

When I need support, I can count on...	
	☐ Optimistic
	☐ Happy
I felt inspired when...	☐ Sad/Tearful
	☐ Uneasy
	☐ Frustrated
I felt happiest when...	☐ Lonely
	☐ Anger
	☐ Tired

I am grateful for...

I felt disrespected/stressed when...

I spoke up when...

I could have done this better...

I know I'm the "man" when...

This was hard but I overcame it by...

The one thing I will do differently tomorrow is...

This is what I will remember most about today:

90-DAYS OF SELF-REFLECTIONS

Date: /   /

	Today I Feel:
When I need support, I can count on...	☐ Optimistic
	☐ Happy
I felt inspired when...	☐ Sad/Tearful
	☐ Uneasy
	☐ Frustrated
I felt happiest when...	☐ Lonely
	☐ Anger
	☐ Tired

I am grateful for...

I felt disrespected/stressed when...

I spoke up when...

I could have done this better...

I know I'm the "man" when...

This was hard but I overcame it by...

The one thing I will do differently tomorrow is...

This is what I will remember most about today:

90-DAYS OF SELF-REFLECTIONS

Date: /   /

	Today I Feel:
When I need support, I can count on...	☐ Optimistic ☐ Happy
I felt inspired when...	☐ Sad/Tearful ☐ Uneasy ☐ Frustrated
I felt happiest when...	☐ Lonely ☐ Anger ☐ Tired

I am grateful for...

I felt disrespected/stressed when...

I spoke up when...

I could have done this better...

I know I'm the "man" when...

This was hard but I overcame it by...

The one thing I will do differently tomorrow is...

This is what I will remember most about today:

90-DAYS OF SELF-REFLECTIONS

Date: /   /

When I need support, I can count on...	Today I Feel:
	☐ Optimistic
	☐ Happy
I felt inspired when...	☐ Sad/Tearful
	☐ Uneasy
	☐ Frustrated
I felt happiest when...	☐ Lonely
	☐ Anger
	☐ Tired

I am grateful for...

I felt disrespected/stressed when...

I spoke up when...

I could have done this better...

I know I'm the "man" when...

This was hard but I overcame it by...

The one thing I will do differently tomorrow is...

This is what I will remember most about today:

90-DAYS OF SELF-REFLECTIONS

Date: /   /

When I need support, I can count on...	**Today I Feel:**
	☐ Optimistic
	☐ Happy
I felt inspired when...	☐ Sad/Tearful
	☐ Uneasy
	☐ Frustrated
I felt happiest when...	☐ Lonely
	☐ Anger
	☐ Tired

I am grateful for...

I felt disrespected/stressed when...

I spoke up when...

I could have done this better...

I know I'm the "man" when...

This was hard but I overcame it by...

The one thing I will do differently tomorrow is...

This is what I will remember most about today:

90-DAYS OF SELF-REFLECTIONS

Date: /   /

When I need support, I can count on...	**Today I Feel:** ☐ Optimistic ☐ Happy ☐ Sad/Tearful ☐ Uneasy ☐ Frustrated ☐ Lonely ☐ Anger ☐ Tired
I felt inspired when...	
I felt happiest when...	

I am grateful for...

I felt disrespected/stressed when...

I spoke up when...

I could have done this better...

I know I'm the "man" when...

This was hard but I overcame it by...

The one thing I will do differently tomorrow is...

This is what I will remember most about today:

90-DAYS OF SELF-REFLECTIONS

Date: /   /

When I need support, I can count on...	**Today I Feel:**
	☐ Optimistic
	☐ Happy
I felt inspired when...	☐ Sad/Tearful
	☐ Uneasy
	☐ Frustrated
I felt happiest when...	☐ Lonely
	☐ Anger
	☐ Tired

I am grateful for...

I felt disrespected/stressed when...

I spoke up when...

I could have done this better...

I know I'm the "man" when...

This was hard but I overcame it by...

The one thing I will do differently tomorrow is...

This is what I will remember most about today:

90-DAYS OF SELF-REFLECTIONS

Date: /   /

When I need support, I can count on...	**Today I Feel:**
	☐ Optimistic
	☐ Happy
I felt inspired when...	☐ Sad/Tearful
	☐ Uneasy
	☐ Frustrated
I felt happiest when...	☐ Lonely
	☐ Anger
	☐ Tired

I am grateful for...

I felt disrespected/stressed when...

I spoke up when...

I could have done this better...

I know I'm the "man" when...

This was hard but I overcame it by...

The one thing I will do differently tomorrow is...

This is what I will remember most about today:

90-DAYS OF SELF-REFLECTIONS

Date: /   /

When I need support, I can count on...	**Today I Feel:**
	☐ Optimistic
	☐ Happy
I felt inspired when...	☐ Sad/Tearful
	☐ Uneasy
	☐ Frustrated
I felt happiest when...	☐ Lonely
	☐ Anger
	☐ Tired

I am grateful for...

I felt disrespected/stressed when...

I spoke up when...

I could have done this better...

I know I'm the "man" when...

This was hard but I overcame it by...

The one thing I will do differently tomorrow is...

This is what I will remember most about today:

90-DAYS OF SELF-REFLECTIONS

Date: /   /

	Today I Feel:
When I need support, I can count on...	☐ Optimistic
	☐ Happy
I felt inspired when...	☐ Sad/Tearful
	☐ Uneasy
	☐ Frustrated
I felt happiest when...	☐ Lonely
	☐ Anger
	☐ Tired

I am grateful for...

I felt disrespected/stressed when...

I spoke up when...

I could have done this better...

I know I'm the "man" when...

This was hard but I overcame it by...

The one thing I will do differently tomorrow is...

This is what I will remember most about today:

90-DAYS OF SELF-REFLECTIONS

Date: / /

	Today I Feel:
When I need support, I can count on...	☐ Optimistic ☐ Happy
I felt inspired when...	☐ Sad/Tearful ☐ Uneasy ☐ Frustrated
I felt happiest when...	☐ Lonely ☐ Anger ☐ Tired

I am grateful for...

I felt disrespected/stressed when...

I spoke up when...

I could have done this better...

I know I'm the "man" when...

This was hard but I overcame it by...

The one thing I will do differently tomorrow is...

This is what I will remember most about today:

90-DAYS OF SELF-REFLECTIONS

Date: /   /

When I need support, I can count on...	**Today I Feel:**
	☐ Optimistic
	☐ Happy
I felt inspired when...	☐ Sad/Tearful
	☐ Uneasy
	☐ Frustrated
I felt happiest when...	☐ Lonely
	☐ Anger
	☐ Tired

I am grateful for...

I felt disrespected/stressed when...

I spoke up when...

I could have done this better...

I know I'm the "man" when...

This was hard but I overcame it by...

The one thing I will do differently tomorrow is...

This is what I will remember most about today:

90-DAYS OF SELF-REFLECTIONS

Date: /   /

	Today I Feel:
When I need support, I can count on...	☐ Optimistic
	☐ Happy
I felt inspired when...	☐ Sad/Tearful
	☐ Uneasy
	☐ Frustrated
I felt happiest when...	☐ Lonely
	☐ Anger
	☐ Tired

I am grateful for...

I felt disrespected/stressed when...

I spoke up when...

I could have done this better...

I know I'm the "man" when...

This was hard but I overcame it by...

The one thing I will do differently tomorrow is...

This is what I will remember most about today:

90-DAYS OF SELF-REFLECTIONS

Date: /   /

	Today I Feel:
When I need support, I can count on...	☐ Optimistic
	☐ Happy
I felt inspired when...	☐ Sad/Tearful
	☐ Uneasy
	☐ Frustrated
I felt happiest when...	☐ Lonely
	☐ Anger
	☐ Tired

I am grateful for...

I felt disrespected/stressed when...

I spoke up when...

I could have done this better...

I know I'm the "man" when...

This was hard but I overcame it by...

The one thing I will do differently tomorrow is...

This is what I will remember most about today:

90-DAYS OF SELF-REFLECTIONS

Date: /   /

When I need support, I can count on...	**Today I Feel:** ☐ Optimistic ☐ Happy
I felt inspired when...	☐ Sad/Tearful ☐ Uneasy ☐ Frustrated
I felt happiest when...	☐ Lonely ☐ Anger ☐ Tired

I am grateful for...

I felt disrespected/stressed when...

I spoke up when...

I could have done this better...

I know I'm the "man" when...

This was hard but I overcame it by...

The one thing I will do differently tomorrow is...

This is what I will remember most about today:

90-DAYS OF SELF-REFLECTIONS

Date: /   /

	Today I Feel:
When I need support, I can count on...	☐ Optimistic
	☐ Happy
I felt inspired when...	☐ Sad/Tearful
	☐ Uneasy
	☐ Frustrated
I felt happiest when...	☐ Lonely
	☐ Anger
	☐ Tired

I am grateful for...

I felt disrespected/stressed when...

I spoke up when...

I could have done this better...

I know I'm the "man" when...

This was hard but I overcame it by...

The one thing I will do differently tomorrow is...

This is what I will remember most about today:

90-DAYS OF SELF-REFLECTIONS

Date: /   /

When I need support, I can count on...	**Today I Feel:**
	☐ Optimistic
	☐ Happy
I felt inspired when...	☐ Sad/Tearful
	☐ Uneasy
	☐ Frustrated
I felt happiest when...	☐ Lonely
	☐ Anger
	☐ Tired

I am grateful for...

I felt disrespected/stressed when...

I spoke up when...

I could have done this better...

I know I'm the "man" when...

This was hard but I overcame it by...

The one thing I will do differently tomorrow is...

This is what I will remember most about today:

90-DAYS OF SELF-REFLECTIONS

Date: /   /

When I need support, I can count on...	**Today I Feel:** ☐ Optimistic ☐ Happy
I felt inspired when...	☐ Sad/Tearful ☐ Uneasy ☐ Frustrated
I felt happiest when...	☐ Lonely ☐ Anger ☐ Tired

I am grateful for...

I felt disrespected/stressed when...

I spoke up when...

I could have done this better...

I know I'm the "man" when...

This was hard but I overcame it by...

The one thing I will do differently tomorrow is...

This is what I will remember most about today:

90-DAYS OF SELF-REFLECTIONS

Date: /   /

When I need support, I can count on...	Today I Feel:
	☐ Optimistic
	☐ Happy
I felt inspired when...	☐ Sad/Tearful
	☐ Uneasy
	☐ Frustrated
I felt happiest when...	☐ Lonely
	☐ Anger
	☐ Tired

I am grateful for...

I felt disrespected/stressed when...

I spoke up when...

I could have done this better...

I know I'm the "man" when...

This was hard but I overcame it by...

The one thing I will do differently tomorrow is...

This is what I will remember most about today:

90-DAYS OF SELF-REFLECTIONS

Date: /   /

When I need support, I can count on...	☐ Optimistic ☐ Happy
I felt inspired when...	☐ Sad/Tearful ☐ Uneasy ☐ Frustrated
I felt happiest when...	☐ Lonely ☐ Anger ☐ Tired

I am grateful for...

I felt disrespected/stressed when...

I spoke up when...

I could have done this better...

I know I'm the "man" when...

This was hard but I overcame it by...

The one thing I will do differently tomorrow is...

This is what I will remember most about today:

90-DAYS OF SELF-REFLECTIONS

Date: / /

	Today I Feel:
When I need support, I can count on...	☐ Optimistic
	☐ Happy
I felt inspired when...	☐ Sad/Tearful
	☐ Uneasy
	☐ Frustrated
I felt happiest when...	☐ Lonely
	☐ Anger
	☐ Tired

I am grateful for...

I felt disrespected/stressed when...

I spoke up when...

I could have done this better...

I know I'm the "man" when...

This was hard but I overcame it by...

The one thing I will do differently tomorrow is...

This is what I will remember most about today:

90-DAYS OF SELF-REFLECTIONS

Date: /   /

	Today I Feel:
When I need support, I can count on...	☐ Optimistic
	☐ Happy
I felt inspired when...	☐ Sad/Tearful
	☐ Uneasy
	☐ Frustrated
I felt happiest when...	☐ Lonely
	☐ Anger
	☐ Tired

I am grateful for...

I felt disrespected/stressed when...

I spoke up when...

I could have done this better...

I know I'm the "man" when...

This was hard but I overcame it by...

The one thing I will do differently tomorrow is...

This is what I will remember most about today:

90-DAYS OF SELF-REFLECTIONS

Date: /   /

When I need support, I can count on...	Today I Feel:

When I need support, I can count on...

Today I Feel:
- ☐ Optimistic
- ☐ Happy
- ☐ Sad/Tearful
- ☐ Uneasy
- ☐ Frustrated
- ☐ Lonely
- ☐ Anger
- ☐ Tired

I felt inspired when...

I felt happiest when...

I am grateful for...

I felt disrespected/stressed when...

I spoke up when...

I could have done this better...

I know I'm the "man" when...

This was hard but I overcame it by...

The one thing I will do differently tomorrow is...

This is what I will remember most about today:

90-DAYS OF SELF-REFLECTIONS

Date: /   /

When I need support, I can count on...	Today I Feel:
	☐ Optimistic
	☐ Happy
I felt inspired when...	☐ Sad/Tearful
	☐ Uneasy
	☐ Frustrated
I felt happiest when...	☐ Lonely
	☐ Anger
	☐ Tired

I am grateful for...

I felt disrespected/stressed when...

I spoke up when...

I could have done this better...

I know I'm the "man" when...

This was hard but I overcame it by...

The one thing I will do differently tomorrow is...

This is what I will remember most about today:

90-DAYS OF SELF-REFLECTIONS

Date: /   /

	Today I Feel:
When I need support, I can count on...	☐ Optimistic
	☐ Happy
I felt inspired when...	☐ Sad/Tearful
	☐ Uneasy
	☐ Frustrated
I felt happiest when...	☐ Lonely
	☐ Anger
	☐ Tired

I am grateful for...

I felt disrespected/stressed when...

I spoke up when...

I could have done this better...

I know I'm the "man" when...

This was hard but I overcame it by...

The one thing I will do differently tomorrow is...

This is what I will remember most about today:

90-DAYS OF SELF-REFLECTIONS

Date: /   /

	Today I Feel:
When I need support, I can count on...	☐ Optimistic
	☐ Happy
I felt inspired when...	☐ Sad/Tearful
	☐ Uneasy
	☐ Frustrated
I felt happiest when...	☐ Lonely
	☐ Anger
	☐ Tired

I am grateful for...

I felt disrespected/stressed when...

I spoke up when...

I could have done this better...

I know I'm the "man" when...

This was hard but I overcame it by...

The one thing I will do differently tomorrow is...

This is what I will remember most about today:

90-DAYS OF SELF-REFLECTIONS

Date: /   /

When I need support, I can count on...	Today I Feel:
	☐ Optimistic
	☐ Happy
I felt inspired when...	☐ Sad/Tearful
	☐ Uneasy
	☐ Frustrated
I felt happiest when...	☐ Lonely
	☐ Anger
	☐ Tired

I am grateful for...

I felt disrespected/stressed when...

I spoke up when...

I could have done this better...

I know I'm the "man" when...

This was hard but I overcame it by...

The one thing I will do differently tomorrow is...

This is what I will remember most about today:

90-DAYS OF SELF-REFLECTIONS

Date: /   /

	Today I Feel:
When I need support, I can count on...	☐ Optimistic
	☐ Happy
I felt inspired when...	☐ Sad/Tearful
	☐ Uneasy
	☐ Frustrated
I felt happiest when...	☐ Lonely
	☐ Anger
	☐ Tired

I am grateful for...

I felt disrespected/stressed when...

I spoke up when...

I could have done this better...

I know I'm the "man" when...

This was hard but I overcame it by...

The one thing I will do differently tomorrow is...

This is what I will remember most about today:

90-DAYS OF SELF-REFLECTIONS

Date: /   /

When I need support, I can count on...	Today I Feel:
	☐ Optimistic
	☐ Happy
I felt inspired when...	☐ Sad/Tearful
	☐ Uneasy
	☐ Frustrated
I felt happiest when...	☐ Lonely
	☐ Anger
	☐ Tired

I am grateful for...

I felt disrespected/stressed when...

I spoke up when...

I could have done this better...

I know I'm the "man" when...

This was hard but I overcame it by...

The one thing I will do differently tomorrow is...

This is what I will remember most about today:

90-DAYS OF SELF-REFLECTIONS

Date: /   /

	Today I Feel:
When I need support, I can count on...	☐ Optimistic ☐ Happy
I felt inspired when...	☐ Sad/Tearful ☐ Uneasy ☐ Frustrated
I felt happiest when...	☐ Lonely ☐ Anger ☐ Tired

I am grateful for...

I felt disrespected/stressed when...

I spoke up when...

I could have done this better...

I know I'm the "man" when...

This was hard but I overcame it by...

The one thing I will do differently tomorrow is...

This is what I will remember most about today:

90-DAYS OF SELF-REFLECTIONS

Date: /   /

When I need support, I can count on...	**Today I Feel:**
	☐ Optimistic
	☐ Happy
I felt inspired when...	☐ Sad/Tearful
	☐ Uneasy
	☐ Frustrated
I felt happiest when...	☐ Lonely
	☐ Anger
	☐ Tired

I am grateful for...

I felt disrespected/stressed when...

I spoke up when...

I could have done this better...

I know I'm the "man" when...

This was hard but I overcame it by...

The one thing I will do differently tomorrow is...

This is what I will remember most about today:

90-DAYS OF SELF-REFLECTIONS

Date: /   /

When I need support, I can count on...	**Today I Feel:**
	☐ Optimistic
	☐ Happy
I felt inspired when...	☐ Sad/Tearful
	☐ Uneasy
	☐ Frustrated
I felt happiest when...	☐ Lonely
	☐ Anger
	☐ Tired

I am grateful for...

I felt disrespected/stressed when...

I spoke up when...

I could have done this better...

I know I'm the "man" when...

This was hard but I overcame it by...

The one thing I will do differently tomorrow is...

This is what I will remember most about today:

90-DAYS OF SELF-REFLECTIONS

Date: /   /

When I need support, I can count on...	Today I Feel:
	☐ Optimistic
	☐ Happy
I felt inspired when...	☐ Sad/Tearful
	☐ Uneasy
	☐ Frustrated
I felt happiest when...	☐ Lonely
	☐ Anger
	☐ Tired

I am grateful for...

I felt disrespected/stressed when...

I spoke up when...

I could have done this better...

I know I'm the "man" when...

This was hard but I overcame it by...

The one thing I will do differently tomorrow is...

This is what I will remember most about today:

90-DAYS OF SELF-REFLECTIONS

Date: /   /

	Today I Feel:
When I need support, I can count on...	☐ Optimistic ☐ Happy
I felt inspired when...	☐ Sad/Tearful ☐ Uneasy ☐ Frustrated
I felt happiest when...	☐ Lonely ☐ Anger ☐ Tired

I am grateful for...

I felt disrespected/stressed when...

I spoke up when...

I could have done this better...

I know I'm the "man" when...

This was hard but I overcame it by...

The one thing I will do differently tomorrow is...

This is what I will remember most about today:

90-DAYS OF SELF-REFLECTIONS

Date: /   /

When I need support, I can count on...	Today I Feel:
	☐ Optimistic
	☐ Happy
I felt inspired when...	☐ Sad/Tearful
	☐ Uneasy
	☐ Frustrated
I felt happiest when...	☐ Lonely
	☐ Anger
	☐ Tired

I am grateful for...

I felt disrespected/stressed when...

I spoke up when...

I could have done this better...

I know I'm the "man" when...

This was hard but I overcame it by...

The one thing I will do differently tomorrow is...

This is what I will remember most about today:

90-DAYS OF SELF-REFLECTIONS

Date: /   /

When I need support, I can count on...	Today I Feel:
	☐ Optimistic
	☐ Happy
I felt inspired when...	☐ Sad/Tearful
	☐ Uneasy
	☐ Frustrated
I felt happiest when...	☐ Lonely
	☐ Anger
	☐ Tired

I am grateful for...

I felt disrespected/stressed when...

I spoke up when...

I could have done this better...

I know I'm the "man" when...

This was hard but I overcame it by...

The one thing I will do differently tomorrow is...

This is what I will remember most about today:

90-DAYS OF SELF-REFLECTIONS

Date: /   /

When I need support, I can count on...	**Today I Feel:**
	☐ Optimistic
	☐ Happy
I felt inspired when...	☐ Sad/Tearful
	☐ Uneasy
	☐ Frustrated
I felt happiest when...	☐ Lonely
	☐ Anger
	☐ Tired

I am grateful for...

I felt disrespected/stressed when...

I spoke up when...

I could have done this better...

I know I'm the "man" when...

This was hard but I overcame it by...

The one thing I will do differently tomorrow is...

This is what I will remember most about today:

90-DAYS OF SELF-REFLECTIONS

Date: /   /

	Today I Feel:
When I need support, I can count on...	☐ Optimistic
	☐ Happy
I felt inspired when...	☐ Sad/Tearful
	☐ Uneasy
	☐ Frustrated
I felt happiest when...	☐ Lonely
	☐ Anger
	☐ Tired

I am grateful for...

I felt disrespected/stressed when...

I spoke up when...

I could have done this better...

I know I'm the "man" when...

This was hard but I overcame it by...

The one thing I will do differently tomorrow is...

This is what I will remember most about today:

90-DAYS OF SELF-REFLECTIONS

Date: /   /

When I need support, I can count on...	Today I Feel:
	☐ Optimistic
	☐ Happy
I felt inspired when...	☐ Sad/Tearful
	☐ Uneasy
	☐ Frustrated
I felt happiest when...	☐ Lonely
	☐ Anger
	☐ Tired

I am grateful for...

I felt disrespected/stressed when...

I spoke up when...

I could have done this better...

I know I'm the "man" when...

This was hard but I overcame it by...

The one thing I will do differently tomorrow is...

This is what I will remember most about today:

90-DAYS OF SELF-REFLECTIONS

Date: /   /

	Today I Feel:
When I need support, I can count on...	☐ Optimistic
	☐ Happy
I felt inspired when...	☐ Sad/Tearful
	☐ Uneasy
	☐ Frustrated
I felt happiest when...	☐ Lonely
	☐ Anger
	☐ Tired

I am grateful for...

I felt disrespected/stressed when...

I spoke up when...

I could have done this better...

I know I'm the "man" when...

This was hard but I overcame it by...

The one thing I will do differently tomorrow is...

This is what I will remember most about today:

90-DAYS OF SELF-REFLECTIONS

Date: /   /

	Today I Feel:
When I need support, I can count on...	☐ Optimistic
	☐ Happy
I felt inspired when...	☐ Sad/Tearful
	☐ Uneasy
	☐ Frustrated
I felt happiest when...	☐ Lonely
	☐ Anger
	☐ Tired

I am grateful for...

I felt disrespected/stressed when...

I spoke up when...

I could have done this better...

I know I'm the "man" when...

This was hard but I overcame it by...

The one thing I will do differently tomorrow is...

This is what I will remember most about today:

90-DAYS OF SELF-REFLECTIONS

Date: /   /

When I need support, I can count on...	**Today I Feel:**
	☐ Optimistic
	☐ Happy
I felt inspired when...	☐ Sad/Tearful
	☐ Uneasy
	☐ Frustrated
I felt happiest when...	☐ Lonely
	☐ Anger
	☐ Tired

I am grateful for...

I felt disrespected/stressed when...

I spoke up when...

I could have done this better...

I know I'm the "man" when...

This was hard but I overcame it by...

The one thing I will do differently tomorrow is...

This is what I will remember most about today:

90-DAYS OF SELF-REFLECTIONS

Date: /   /

	Today I Feel:
When I need support, I can count on...	☐ Optimistic ☐ Happy
I felt inspired when...	☐ Sad/Tearful ☐ Uneasy ☐ Frustrated
I felt happiest when...	☐ Lonely ☐ Anger ☐ Tired

I am grateful for...

I felt disrespected/stressed when...

I spoke up when...

I could have done this better...

I know I'm the "man" when...

This was hard but I overcame it by...

The one thing I will do differently tomorrow is...

This is what I will remember most about today:

90-DAYS OF SELF-REFLECTIONS

Date: /   /

	Today I Feel:
When I need support, I can count on...	☐ Optimistic
	☐ Happy
I felt inspired when...	☐ Sad/Tearful
	☐ Uneasy
	☐ Frustrated
I felt happiest when...	☐ Lonely
	☐ Anger
	☐ Tired

I am grateful for...

I felt disrespected/stressed when...

I spoke up when...

I could have done this better...

I know I'm the "man" when...

This was hard but I overcame it by...

The one thing I will do differently tomorrow is...

This is what I will remember most about today:

90-DAYS OF SELF-REFLECTIONS

Date: /   /

	Today I Feel:
When I need support, I can count on...	☐ Optimistic ☐ Happy
I felt inspired when...	☐ Sad/Tearful ☐ Uneasy ☐ Frustrated
I felt happiest when...	☐ Lonely ☐ Anger ☐ Tired

I am grateful for...

I felt disrespected/stressed when...

I spoke up when...

I could have done this better...

I know I'm the "man" when...

This was hard but I overcame it by...

The one thing I will do differently tomorrow is...

This is what I will remember most about today:

90-DAYS OF SELF-REFLECTIONS

Date: /   /

When I need support, I can count on...	**Today I Feel:**
	☐ Optimistic
	☐ Happy
I felt inspired when...	☐ Sad/Tearful
	☐ Uneasy
	☐ Frustrated
I felt happiest when...	☐ Lonely
	☐ Anger
	☐ Tired

I am grateful for...

I felt disrespected/stressed when...

I spoke up when...

I could have done this better...

I know I'm the "man" when...

This was hard but I overcame it by...

The one thing I will do differently tomorrow is...

This is what I will remember most about today:

90-DAYS OF SELF-REFLECTIONS

Date: /   /

When I need support, I can count on...	**Today I Feel:**
	☐ Optimistic
	☐ Happy
I felt inspired when...	☐ Sad/Tearful
	☐ Uneasy
	☐ Frustrated
I felt happiest when...	☐ Lonely
	☐ Anger
	☐ Tired

I am grateful for...

I felt disrespected/stressed when...

I spoke up when...

I could have done this better...

I know I'm the "man" when...

This was hard but I overcame it by...

The one thing I will do differently tomorrow is...

This is what I will remember most about today:

90-DAYS OF SELF-REFLECTIONS

Date: /   /

	Today I Feel:
When I need support, I can count on...	☐ Optimistic
	☐ Happy
I felt inspired when...	☐ Sad/Tearful
	☐ Uneasy
	☐ Frustrated
I felt happiest when...	☐ Lonely
	☐ Anger
	☐ Tired

I am grateful for...

I felt disrespected/stressed when...

I spoke up when...

I could have done this better...

I know I'm the "man" when...

This was hard but I overcame it by...

The one thing I will do differently tomorrow is...

This is what I will remember most about today:

90-DAYS OF SELF-REFLECTIONS

Date: /   /

When I need support, I can count on...	**Today I Feel:** ☐ Optimistic ☐ Happy ☐ Sad/Tearful ☐ Uneasy ☐ Frustrated ☐ Lonely ☐ Anger ☐ Tired
I felt inspired when...	
I felt happiest when...	

I am grateful for...

I felt disrespected/stressed when...

I spoke up when...

I could have done this better...

I know I'm the "man" when...

This was hard but I overcame it by...

The one thing I will do differently tomorrow is...

This is what I will remember most about today:

90-DAYS OF SELF-REFLECTIONS

Date: /   /

When I need support, I can count on...	Today I Feel:
	☐ Optimistic
	☐ Happy
I felt inspired when...	☐ Sad/Tearful
	☐ Uneasy
	☐ Frustrated
I felt happiest when...	☐ Lonely
	☐ Anger
	☐ Tired

I am grateful for...

I felt disrespected/stressed when...

I spoke up when...

I could have done this better...

I know I'm the "man" when...

This was hard but I overcame it by...

The one thing I will do differently tomorrow is...

This is what I will remember most about today:

OTHER GUIDED JOURNALS & DIARIES
— by —
KINYATTA E. GRAY

I Miss You...

Daily Writing Prompts for Reflection, Remembrance, and Spirit Renewal

Fashionista's Travel Diary

A Guided Travel Diary for Travel Planning & Reflections

I'm Doing Me

The Ultimate Breakup Diary for Venting, Reflection & Spirit Renewal

While I'm Still Here

A Guided Expression Journal of Life, Love and Legacy for Those Preparing to Transition

My Crazy Teenage Life

The Ultimate Expression Diary for Venting, Self-Reflections and Self-Love

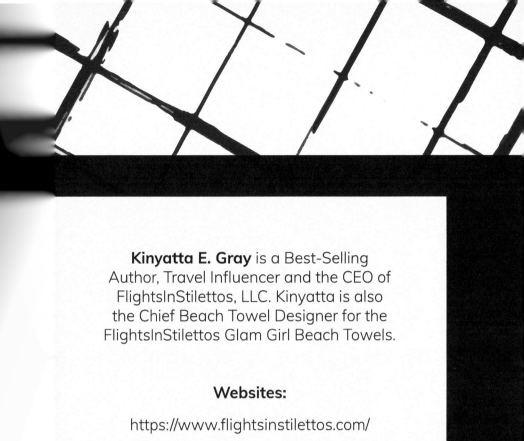

Kinyatta E. Gray is a Best-Selling Author, Travel Influencer and the CEO of FlightsInStilettos, LLC. Kinyatta is also the Chief Beach Towel Designer for the FlightsInStilettos Glam Girl Beach Towels.

Websites:

https://www.flightsinstilettos.com/

https://www.kinyattagray.com/

https://www.honoringmissbee.com/

CPSIA information can be obtained
at www.ICGtesting.com
Printed in the USA
BVHW051120051021
618160BV00005B/40